HEY, I'M JENN

Firstly, I want to say a big thank you f̶ ̶̶̶̶,̶ ̶̶g this workbook. To give you a bit of background about me, I run the award-winning wedding business called The Handmade Sign Company, which specialises in calligraphy wedding signage, however I create lots of hand lettered makes for all occasions! Prior to setting up my business in January 2019 I was a graphic designer for over 14 years, which is where I found my initial love for typography design, however I was never any good at it at the time! Instead I always admired hand lettering from a distance and just played around with it from time to time.

However, after battling postnatal depression after my 2nd daughter was born in 2017, I started to take it more seriously and I was soon practicing every night. It was an incredibly therapeutic way to de-stress, and I strongly believe it was a key factor in helping me overcome the illness, and the main reason I got into teaching others the craft.

Since those early days practicing, I now get to create hand lettered items for so many amazing couples on their special day, and I feel incredibly honoured to get to do what I love every day!

I hope you find this book useful whilst starting out on your lettering journey! Just remember, learning modern lettering is not a race, enjoy the process, be patient with yourself and have fun!

jenn x

To Sofia and Helena, my beautiful girls

You are my greatest achievement, the loves of my life and without you, none of this would have been possible. Thank you for showing me unconditional love every day.

Mummy x

First published in 2020.

ISBN 978 1 5272 6136 5

Book design by Jennifer Cabrelli.

Published by The Handmade Sign Company
www.handmadesigncompany.co.uk

CONTENTS

WHAT IS MODERN LETTERING?

You may have heard of lots of names for modern lettering like modern calligraphy, brush lettering and hand lettering to name a few. I personally don't think it matters what you call it but traditionally, the term calligraphy refers to work created with a nib and ink, whereas brush lettering is done with a brush and ink or brush pens. However, in my opinion, no style of lettering is better than the other so I don't think it really matters. My personal style of lettering is more recognisable as a modern calligraphy style, whether I use a nib or not, but I tend to call it modern lettering as it's a broader term.

HOW DOES MODERN CALLIGRAPHY DIFFER FROM TRADITIONAL CALLIGRAPHY?

Modern calligraphy is a very different style in comparison to traditional calligraphy. In traditional, there are a number of rules or guidelines that dictate how you must write your letters. These rules will differ depending on what type of calligraphy you are using, but on average they tend to state your lettering must be in a straight line, every letter must be the same height as the next, and you must only ever write at a 45 degree angle. Before I found my passion for modern calligraphy, I initially tried to follow these rules in the pieces I created. Now time for some honesty... I am a massive perfectionist! I over scrutinise everything I do, and when I tried to follow these rules, I definitely did not find it at all like the relaxing craft I do today! What I liked about modern calligraphy was how I could just enjoy the freedom of writing, and developing my own style. In simple terms, modern calligraphy is a much more fun, bouncy, free-flowing version of traditional calligraphy.

MY HAND LETTERING IS AWFUL, CAN I STILL LEARN TO LETTER?

Yes! More honesty... my handwriting is appalling! To the point where I get embarrassed when I make notes around other people because I suddenly realise if they look at it, they would never believe I really do the calligraphy on my signs by hand! So I promise, no matter how terrible you think your handwriting is, you can learn to letter as it's a very different process.

A NOTE TO THE LEFTIES

I have run many face-to-face lettering workshops, and at every one I always have at least one or two left-handed learners, who are often concerned they may not be able to learn to letter. But don't be, it definitely is possible! What I have come to find is every person will have their own way of writing, and you just need to find which is the most natural for you. Some people write by writing from above and bending their wrist over the top of their work, whereas others come from underneath. Some change how they position their paper in front of them and some even write backwards (just don't ask me how, I am always amazed when I see those that do it that way)! Just keep practicing with different positions and you will find what works for you.

JOIN OUR LETTERING COMMUNITY

Before you get started, make sure you head over to my members only Facebook group to ask any questions, get support on your lettering and find extra hints, tips and tutorials at **www.facebook.com/groups/hscletteringcommunity**.

TERMINOLOGY

I try and avoid being jargony (I hate it myself!) but there will be some terms that you will need to know before we get started.

1   **Hairline.** The thinnest line possible. Upstrokes and horizontal lines are hairlines.

2   **Upstroke.** Any stroke that moves up; always a hairline.

3   **Downstroke.** Any stroke that moves down; apply pressure to achieve.

4   **Ascender.** A portion of a lowercase letter that extends above the midline.

5   **Descender.** A portion of a letter that descends below the baseline, such as a lowercase g, j, p and y.

6   **Baseline.** The baseline is the invisible line where your letters sit. While these letters may have descenders that dip below the line, the main body of the letters all rest here.

7   **Midline.** This is the invisible line that runs along the tops of the main body of lowercase letters, excluding ascenders.

8   **Capital/Ascender line.** This is the invisible line that runs along the top of capital letters and ascenders.

9   **Descender line.** This is the invisible line that runs along the bottom of descenders.

Ascender — Capital/ Ascender Line — Midline — Downstroke — Upstroke — Baseline — Descender — Descender Line

TYPES OF LETTERING

CALLIGRAPHY

Done with a nib and ink, the letters have thick downstrokes and thin upstrokes to create the recognisable calligraphy style.

FAUX CALLIGRAPHY

Sometimes, due to the scale of work or material you are using a nib isn't possible, so faux calligraphy is usually done with a round-tipped pen by first writing out the letters and then going back over the down strokes to thicken them up.

MONOLINE CALLIGRAPHY

Monoline again uses a round tipped pen, and instead of going back over the letters like in faux calligraphy, you leave it as the one line.

BRUSH LETTERING

Brush lettering is done either with a paintbrush or brush pen, and often produces a thicker style than a nib. There are lots of different styles to brush lettering and this is just one example of what can be achieved.

BLOCK LETTERING

This lettering is commonly used as a supporting style with the above. There are thousands of styles and ways to experiment with block lettering.

BLOCK LETTERING

MY FAVOURITE TOOLS

When starting out, you'll see lots of tools online to buy, there's tonnes of nibs, brush pens, brushes, markers, paints, inks, and depending on what style of lettering you are most interested in will also determine which tools you will need.

In this guide, I have listed all of the tools you will need for any of the different types of lettering. My recommendation would be to try as many as you can to see what you like and don't like, but don't do what I did and buy loads of stuff because that's what you see everyone else using so it must be perfect. Everyone is different, and what works for some may not necessarily work for others. So experiment where you can, but to begin with, my absolute favourite tool to learn with is also the cheapest - a pencil. This basic tool is perfect for learning pressure and the basic shapes of modern calligraphy which you can then translate into either nib and ink, brush pens or faux calligraphy.

WHAT ELSE DO I NEED FOR USING THIS GUIDE?

As well as the pencil, the other tools you will need for starting out with this guide are:

- A trusty eraser! (That's also what I like about the pencil.. you can rub it out if it all goes wrong!)
- Paper (simple copier paper will suffice)
- Tracing paper

Additional tools will also be needed for each of the projects at the end of this guide, and the tools for each of these are listed in each tutorial.

OTHER TOOLS TO TRY AS YOU DEVELOP

Once you have learnt the basics with the pencil, you may then wish to try some of the other tools on the market; I have listed some of the most popular below. You will also find a handy resources section at the back of this guide on where to purchase these materials.

- **Brush pens** – Tombow Dual brush pen and Pentel Fude Touch Sign Pen are the most popular ones. These have a flexible nib that create a thin upstroke and thick downstroke when you vary the pressure.
- **Brushes** – small round brushes size 2, larger rounded brushes are useful for sign painting and brush lettering with ink.
- **Inks** – there are lots on the market. As the majority of work that I do is sign writing, I don't tend to use many myself, but when I do I use Daler Rowney Fw Acrylic Artists Ink, or Winsor & Newton inks which are very accessible in most stationery stores.
- **Other pens and markers** – fine liners, gel pens and paint pens are all essential tools for faux calligraphy and monoline lettering. Posca pens are by far the most popular paint pens and come in a wide range of nib sizes and shapes for different purposes.
- **Paper** – If you are using a pencil, brush pens or round pens, then every day copier paper will do for practicing on. However if you are using calligraphy nibs, or brushes with inks, then you'll need some high quality paper otherwise the ink just tends to bleed. A layout pad or Rhodia paper is usually good for calligraphy as it's smooth and quite thin, allowing you to place guidelines behind the page for when you are practicing or developing a composition.

1. Paintbrush (for wood prep)
2. Wide Flat Paintbrush (for washes)
3. Size 1 Round Paintbrush
4. Size 2 Round Paintbrush
5. Pencil
6. POSCA PC-5M
7. POSCA PC-1M
8. Molotow One4All Acrylic
9. Uni Paint Marker
10. Tombow Dual Brush Pen
11. Tombow Fudenosuke Brush Pen
12. Pentel Touch Sign Brush Pen
13. Uni-Ball Pin Fine Liner
14. Uni-Ball Signo Broad
15. Calligraphy Penholder
16. Chalk
17. Ink and Calligraphy Nibs

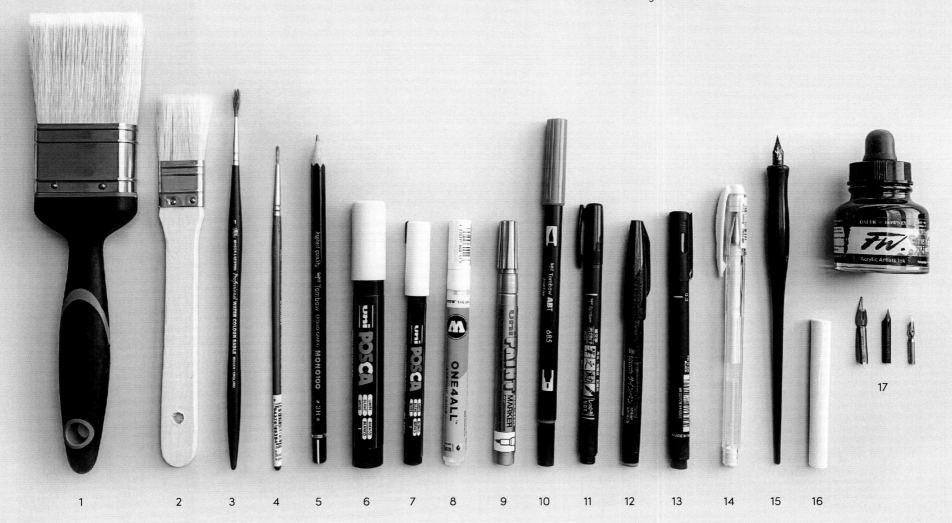

1 2 3 4 5 6 7 8 9 10 11 12 13 14 15 16

WELCOME TO
THE WEDDING OF

Dani
& Matt

25TH APRIL 2019

Photo: Pear and Bear Photography / www.pearbearphotography.com

WHERE TO BEGIN

So now you have the tools you need, you are ready to get started on your lettering journey!

If you begin by picking up your pencil, and on a scrap piece of paper try drawing some short 45 degree lines. Now vary your pressure to achieve different thicknesses of line. Also try adjusting your grip to see what feels the most natural to you. I typically hold the pencil quite low down to the tip, which helps me get greater variances in pressure. If you try holding the pencil high up, you will notice you can't get as much control.

TIP: When using a fresh pencil, I recommend scribbling on some scrap paper to blunt the tip slightly which will help you achieve the thicker downstrokes!

SPEED

It is natural when we are writing to try and write as quickly as possible, but with lettering it is best to do the opposite. The slower you go, the more control you will have creating the letters. Think of it more as drawing the letters rather than writing.

PRACTICE

The last top tip to mention is that lettering is not something that most people pick up first time round. The more you practice the better you will get, so don't get disheartened if you find it harder than you expect on your first try...keep at it and you will see improvements! I always suggest keeping your older work and comparing to it as time goes on and you will be surprised by the difference!

DRILLS

Overleaf you'll find a page of drills. These don't look very exciting, but these basic shapes are what teaches our hands to make the right movements that eventually form the letters of the alphabet. If you do these every day, eventually they become second nature, and the more confident you get with these the better you will become at your letters. Even today, when starting a new job, I will do 5 minutes of drills to warm up my hand and wrist before starting.

Now, let's get started! Lay over a sheet of tracing paper to trace the shapes, adding more pressure for your downstrokes, and less pressure for the upstrokes. On each of the shapes are guides to show you where to start with your pencil.

TIP: For your thin upstrokes just very lightly glide the tip of the pencil over the paper rather than pressing down.

Once you feel confident tracing these, why not give them a go freehand? Once you feel happy you have grasped the changes in pressure for the different shapes, then move on to the next section.

TIP: You don't need to create the shapes and letters in one fluid movement. Feel free to lift your pencil off and start again, but try to always lift at the end of a downstroke as its hard to create a fluid line on an upstroke.

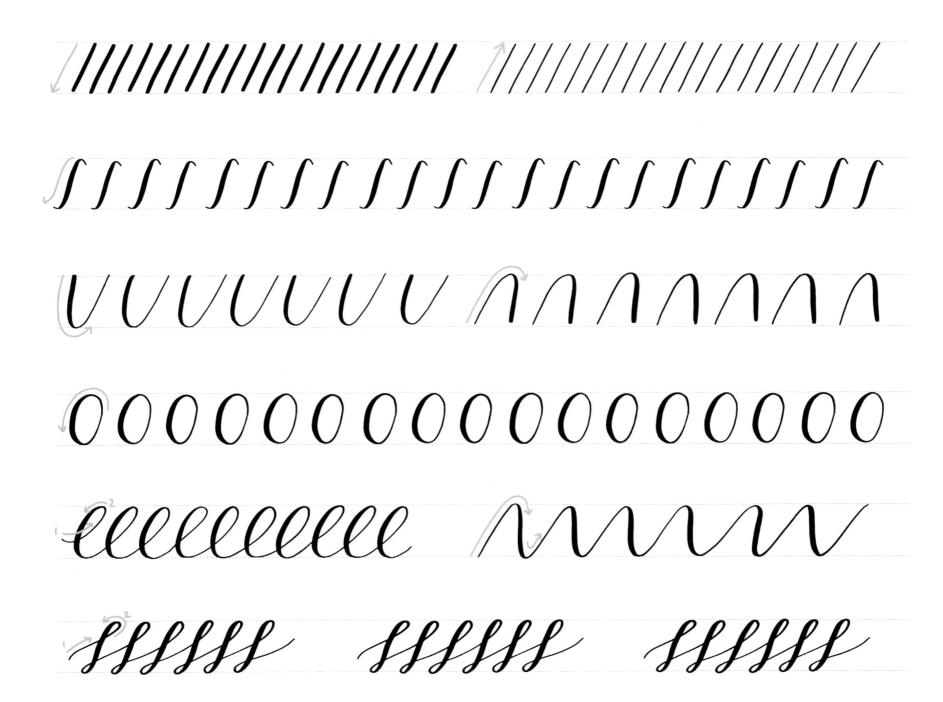

THROW *petals & wishes* FOR THE NEW *M & MRS*

VINS VOURLES

L & M

WELCOME TO OUR
unplugged
ceremony

PLEASE TURN OFF
YOUR CAMERAS AND
MOBILE PHONES AND
JUST BE OUR GUEST
THE PHOTOGRAPHERS HERE
WILL HANDLE THE REST

thank you

CALLIGRAPHY ALPHABET: LOWERCASE

The calligraphy alphabet is recognisable with it's thin upstrokes and thick downstrokes.

Trace the letter shapes by following the arrows and then try your own using the space to the right.

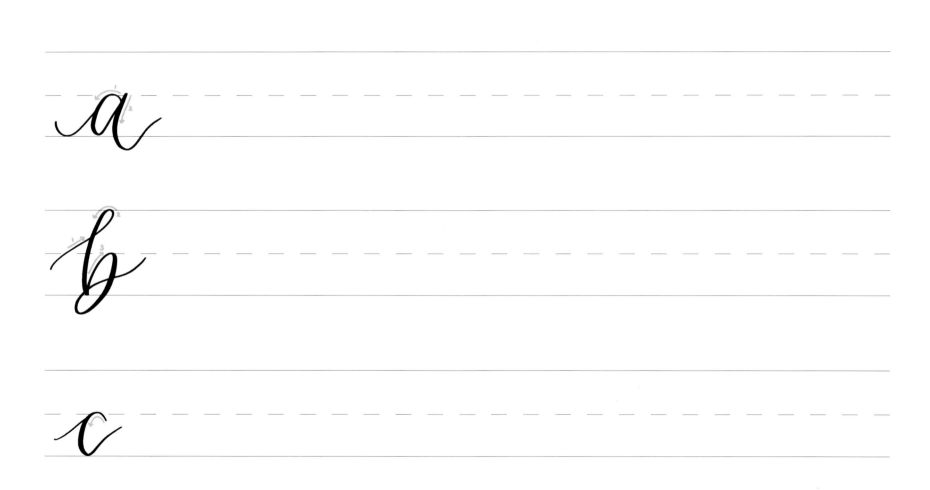

d

e

f

g

l

m

n

o

p

q

r

s

t

u

v

w

NEED ANY ADVICE?

Join my members only Facebook group to ask any questions, and get support on your lettering as well as extra hints, tips and tutorials – www.facebook.com/groups/hsletteringcommunity

CALLIGRAPHY ALPHABET: UPPERCASE

Using uppercase letters is entirely a personal preference. I personally don't use them unless the design calls for it, or the client requests it as I prefer how my lettering looks all in lowercase. But should you wish to use them, here are the uppercase letters for you to practice.

H

I

J

K

P

Q

R

S

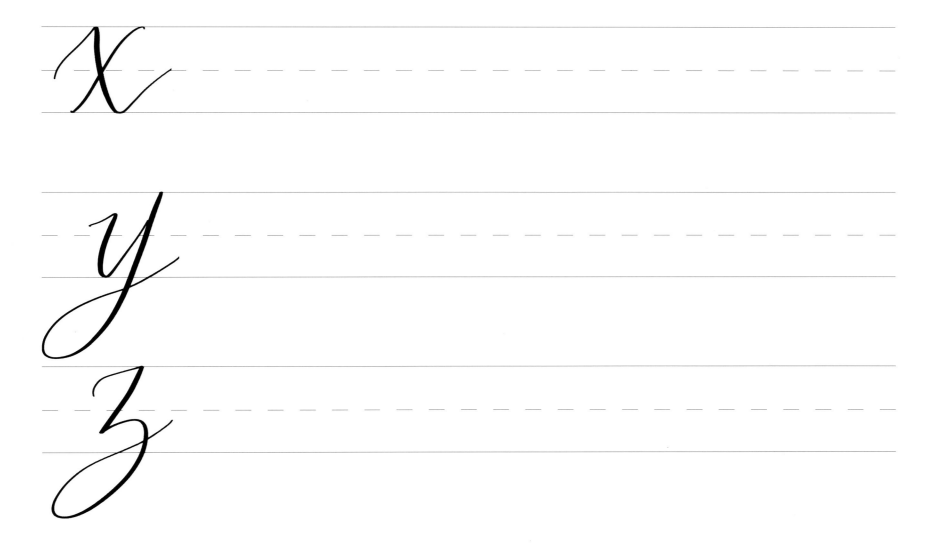

NEED ANY ADVICE?

Join my members only Facebook group to ask any questions, and get support on your lettering as well as extra hints, tips and tutorials – www.facebook.com/groups/hsletteringcommunity

CALLIGRAPHY ALPHABET: NUMBER REFERENCE GUIDE

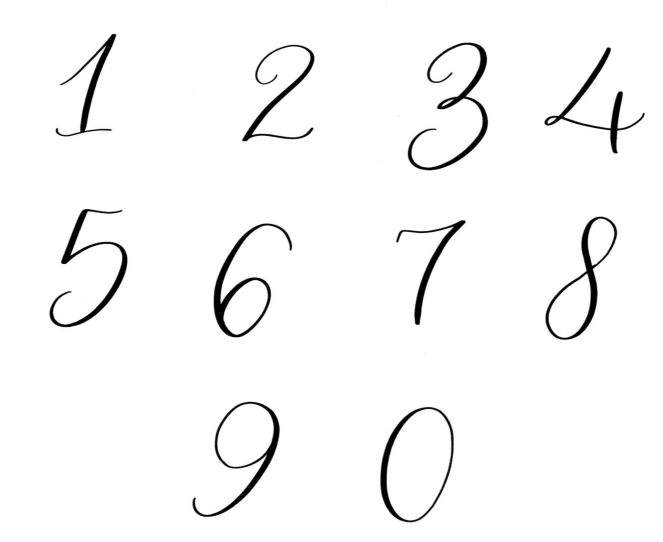

PRACTICE

FAUX CALLIGRAPHY ALPHABET

Faux calligraphy works in the same way as calligraphy, but because it is done with a round pointed pen you cannot achieve the thick downstrokes. Instead it is necessary to go back over the downstrokes and manually thicken them up, and colour the space in as shown.

FAUX CALLIGRAPHY PRACTICE

Using your pencil (without any change in pressure) or a round pointed pen, give faux calligraphy a try yourself.

PRACTICE

FORMING WORDS

Now on to writing some actual words. Joining letters into words is one of the hardest parts of modern calligraphy, but once you start seeing how they can connect, it gets easier! One key thing to remember, is you don't have to write the word in one fluid motion. Lift the pencil up when needed – just avoid doing so on a hairline upstroke, or on a curved shape as this will stop your letters flowing.

Start by looking at this example, and notice how the letters connect to each other.

PRACTICE JOINING YOUR NAME

Now have a practice writing your name. I always find this is a good starting point as most of us don't have to think too much when writing our own name, and so you can instead focus on how the letters would connect. If you can't work out how a letter connects, write them out separately and then you can look at where the end of one letter can join to the next, then try writing it out fully to get a natural flow in your writing.

PRACTICE

Now have a try joining some of these other words together.

happy

PRACTICE

Now have a try joining some of these other words together.

love

PRACTICE

Now have a try joining some of these other words together.

Wedding

PRACTICE

Now have a try joining some of your own words together.

HOW DO I MAKE MY LETTERS BOUNCE?

Once you are comfortable with your letters and connecting them to form words, you can start to play around with them and develop your own style. One that is really popular, which is a more recognisable style with modern calligraphy is how the letters seem to 'bounce'. This is where, instead of writing all your letters on a baseline as we have done up until this point, you over extend the descenders and ascenders, and tweak the size of other letters to make them all flow into each other. This may sound easy, but it can take a while to get the hang of, and I would definitely recommend you feel 100% comfortable with the previous steps before moving on to this section.

To explain more about what I mean by bounce, here is an example. When I add bounce to my lettering, instead of using a baseline, I try to make sure the middle of each letter passes through a midline so the word still looks like its in a straight line.

EVOLUTION OF YOUR STYLE

The more you letter, the more your style will develop and evolve, and this never changes. Even now I am still changing different elements of my personal style. A good tip is to record all of your lettering so you can look back to see how much your lettering has improved, and how it has evolved since you began. Here is an example of how my own lettering has changed since I first started.

One important thing to remember, is even though looking back at my April 2016 piece now, I can see how much my style has evolved, I remember being proud of that piece. So proud that I shared it on my social media and sent it to all my friends and family, and that's all that matters.

April 2016

March 2020

DEVELOPING YOUR STYLE

The thing I love about modern calligraphy is you can completely experiment and find your own style. I have a variety of styles of lettering depending on the piece I am creating, and each one is constantly evolving. Here are a few examples of how the same word can look different.

PRACTICE

Use this space to practice different styles

ADDING FLOURISHES TO
YOUR LETTERS

Flourishing is basically another word for embellishing your letters, and they can very quickly transform your lettering into something spectacular! They can be simple or complex. I personally, use only simple flourishes, as my style doesn't necessarily suit extravagant ones, and I often find they distract from the overall look I try to achieve. You can flourish single words, or also multiple words as a way to connect them together.

You can also use flourishes to connect letters, my favourite being the 't' and 'h'. Over time, the more you practice, you will develop your own style and find what feels most natural to you.

Because a flourish is something added on to a letter you want to be careful not to compromise the legibility of that letter. For that reason, flourishes are typically only added to ascenders, descenders, t crossbars, ends of words or under words. Certain letters lend themselves more to flourishes, so I have shown a few examples of these.

Have a practice adding some simpler flourishes to your lettering. Keep in mind that any flourishes you add should be based on oval shapes, which help make them feel more fluid, natural and elegant, rather than a bit choppy or random.

PRACTICE

Now have a try flourishing some of your letters.

HOW TO CREATE A STRONG LAYOUT

Coming from a design background, creating a well structured layout and composition is fundamental when I letter a new piece. I want to make sure the most important information stands out where needed, whilst also ensuring the design is well balanced and easy to read.

When starting on a larger design, the first thing to do is write out the words on a piece of paper and work out which words you want to emphasise. This is called design hierarchy. For example, in this portrait wedding welcome sign, I chose to emphasise the names, so I wrote these in calligraphy. Whereas the words 'to the wedding of' and the date of the wedding are secondary information, so I wrote these in a block letter.

Another simple way to ensure your design is easy to read is by ensuring your lettering has plenty of space around it. You don't want any words bumping in to each other or it will just look messy and confusing.

Lots of calligraphy in one space can also look overwhelming, as it is typically much harder to read, so by breaking up larger pieces with different styles of lettering can help readers digest the information faster, which is why I often like to introduce a block lettering style to most of my designs.

WELCOME TO
THE WEDDING OF

Will & Jess

13TH SEPTEMBER 2020

White space to allow the design to breathe and make it easier to read.

Calligraphy adds focus to the most important element of the design.

Block lettering breaks up the design and makes the overall design easier to read.

BLOCK LETTER

A cursive style of writing like modern calligraphy typically sits best with more contemporary lettering styles, whether they be **serif** (for a more traditional feel) or **sans-serif** (for a more modern feel).

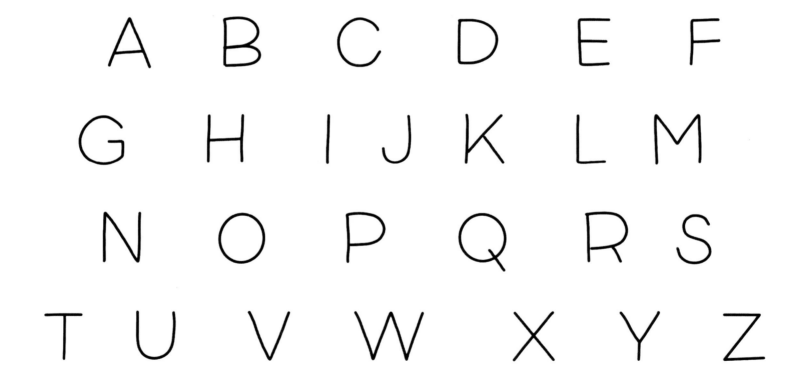

BLOCK LETTER

If you are unsure on what style would be right, you can use the fonts on your own computer for inspiration. Try printing a few out and trying to replicate them. This is how I originally learnt how to write block letters by breaking down how digital fonts were structured.

TIP

Guidelines are incredibly useful when block lettering!

Aa Bb Cc Dd Ee
Ff Gg Hh Ii Jj Kk
Ll Mm Nn Oo Pp
Qq Rr Ss Tt Uu
Vv Ww Xx Yy Zz

DIDOT TYPEFACE

Aa Bb Cc Dd Ee
Ff Gg Hh Ii Jj Kk
Ll Mm Nn Oo Pp
Qq Rr Ss Tt Uu
Vv Ww Xx Yy Zz

CALISTO MT TYPEFACE

COMMON MISTAKES

GOING TOO FAST

It is important to remember that most of the videos you see on social media are not realtime. Calligraphy is much slower than your usual speed for handwriting. If you are finding you are struggling to get control over your letters, thin upstrokes and consistency then try slowing your lettering down to help you focus on getting a consistent thickness and spacing. Faster strokes are only required for other things such as flourishes.

NOT LIFTING THE PEN

As I have mentioned earlier in this book, you don't need to write all of your letters in one motion like you would when using your normal cursive handwriting. With calligraphy you should stop after each stroke and then lift your pen, which will help you with the consistency and the precision of your strokes.

COMPARISON

I was the worst for comparing my lettering to others when I first started, however when I learnt to just embrace my own style I became much more confident which helped me to improve faster. Whilst admiring other lettering artists work is great for inspiration, it should be just that. Everyone is at a different point in their lettering journey, and you shouldn't give yourself unrealistic expectations and compare your work to anyone elses. Learn to have fun, try out different styles and enjoy the process, and you will see improvement!

TOP TIPS

A common mistake with the O shape is starting on the down stroke which creates a harsh join between the thick and thin strokes. Instead start at 2 o'clock to get a nice transition.

Make sure no thick strokes cross another thick stroke, for example in the letter t.

THE KEY POINTS TO REMEMBER ARE:

- Thick strokes should always be made by going down.
- Thin strokes go up or across.
- A thick stroke should never cross another thick stroke.
- A thin stroke can cross another thin stroke or a thick stroke.

PROJECT ONE

Welcome Sign

Looking to welcome your guests to your big day? A welcome sign is one of the most popular items of signage to have at a wedding, and can be a great way to add personality to your big day. One of the easiest materials to use for a welcome sign is plywood. You can source this fairly easily at your local DIY store, and most will even cut it to size for you.

SUPPLIES

Plywood, cut to size

Sanding sheet

Wood stain of your choice and large soft brush

Scrap paper and pencil

Chalk

Ruler

Low tack masking tape or laser level

Uni POSCA Marker (medium bullet tip)

Paper towel

Wood varnish (optional)

PROCESS

1/ Make sure your piece of wood is of a smooth finish, and all the edges have been sanded down. Clean off any dust from the wood, and using a large brush, apply the stain as per the instructions on the pot. Allow each side to dry before moving on to the next to avoid any unwanted marks and lines. Avoid applying the stain too thickly and instead do multiple coats to get your desired finish.

2/ Using some scrap paper and a pencil, sketch out the general layout you want to go for. I start by drawing basic thumbnail drawings to work out what wording I would like in calligraphy and which bits would look better in block writing. Once you know what you want to do, lightly sketch out your design on the stained piece of wood using your piece of chalk. You can use a laser level or low tack masking tape and a ruler to help you create straight lines if required.

3/ Once you are happy with your design in chalk, it's time to trace over your design with your Uni POSCA pen. Shake your pen thoroughly, and press the nib down on some scrap paper to get the paint flowing through the pen. The chalk can occasionally dry out your pens, so use a paper towel to remove some excess chalk if required, and regularly remove any dust from your pen on to some scrap paper. If you want a faux calligraphy style, wait for the paint to dry before going back over and thickening up your downstrokes.

4/ Once the lettering is dry you can buff away any remaining chalk residue with a dry paper towel. The great thing about Uni POSCA pens is once dry they become waterproof on most materials. However if your sign is intended for outdoor use, I usually play extra safe and protect with a protective spray or clear varnish for extra durability in bad weather.

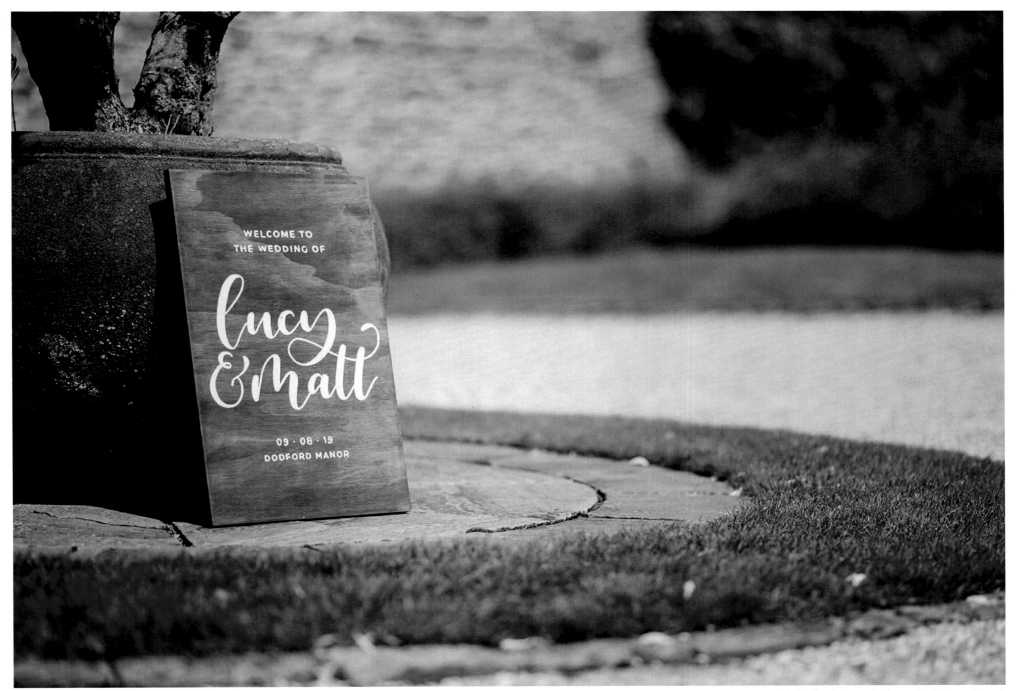

WELCOME TO
THE WEDDING OF

lucy
& Matt

09 · 08 · 19
DODFORD MANOR

PROJECT TWO

pallet name places

Pallet name places are a beautiful touch to a rustic table setting, and can be finished in so many different ways to fit with your theme. There are many different thicknesses of pallet boards available. I am lucky to have an excellent wood reclaim yard near me (I have listed the nationwide group in the resources section so you can see if there is one near you), or you can often source pallets on facebook marketplace. You can then chop the slats down to any size you desire and stain or paint them in any finish of your choice.

SUPPLIES

Reclaimed pallet boards
Sanding sheets or electric sander
Wood saw
Wood stain (optional)
Uni POSCA Marker (fine bullet tip)

PROCESS

1/ If you have a full pallet rather than individual slats, I strongly recommend using your wood saw and cutting them off rather than trying to break the pallet down as they can be very difficult to dismantle without snapping. Once you have your individual boards, you may need to give your pallet a good clean, and I also find it easier at this stage to sand the boards down, before cutting to size (as otherwise they become quite fiddly!).

2/ Once sanded and clean, use your wood saw to cut these down to your desired size. I typically do small and thin ones like pictured, or squares which make great keepsakes for your guests.

3/ Once you have chopped down your boards, use your sanding sheets to sand down the edges. You can then use a wood stain or paint if you wish. I personally really like the bare look!

4/ Once the stain/paint is dry, using your Uni POSCA pen, using either a monoline or faux calligraphy style, write your guests name on the front. If you prefer you can write in chalk first and rub this away once the pen has dried.

PROJECT THREE

Acrylic seating plan

Seating plans are a big part of the wedding celebrations, and they need to be clear and easy to read so there's no drama for your guests finding their seats for the all important speeches. Table plans also look amazing on a huge variety of different materials from acrylic, mirror, pallets or even on old jars and vases; get creative and create something unique! This tutorial tells you how to approach a table plan on acrylic, but the same process can work with whichever material you decide on.

It can be hard to work out what size acrylic to go for. The most popular size I work with is 80 x 60cm which is great for 80-120 guests. Or anything smaller than that can fit on a medium size 60 x 40cm. Ultimately you can fit on most sizes but you just have to adjust your lettering size, so keep that in mind.

SUPPLIES

Large piece of acrylic
Scrap paper and pencil
Ruler
Low tack masking tape
Laser level (optional)
Glass cleaner
Dry cloth
Uni POSCA Markers

PROCESS

1/ The key to seating plans is lots of preparation. Using a pencil and some scrap paper, plan out your table plan layout. You will need to work out the best spacing and text size to make sure all of the names will fit on.

2/ Once you have planned out your spacing and sizing on paper, you should begin by cleaning your acrylic sheet. If they arrived with a protective film (usually on both sides), remove this and using glass cleaner and a dry cloth give both sides a clean to remove any sticky residue from the film. Starting from the top work down the acrylic with a ruler and low tack masking tape to mark out your guidelines.

3/ Using your Uni POSCA pen, write out your design. Once dry you can wipe gently with a dry cloth, or, if you make a mistake and you are using a clear acrylic, you can simply remove using the glass cleaner and start again! (Frosted acrylic typically isn't as forgiving!)

4/ TOP TIP: If centrally aligning your guests names, you can use a laser level to highlight the center guide, and then write from the middle letter, working backwards. For example, for the name JAMES you would write the letter 'M' on the center guide, then write A and J and the E and S.

Welcome

PLEASE FIND YOUR SEAT

A

ALISON ANDREWS...........1
TIMOTHY ANDREWS...........1
SARAH ANDREWS...........2
MARK ANDREWS...........2
CLAIRE ANDREWS...........2
JONATHAN ANDREWS...........5
JOSHUA ANDREWS...........5
EMILY ANDREWS...........5

B

JASON BELL...........
JESSICA BELL...........3
PAUL BARKER...........3
MARIE BARKER...........2
SUE BROWN...........
MARK BROWN...........4

M

PAIGE MILLER...........3
PAUL MILLER...........3
ADAM MILLER...........3

N

STACIE NORRIS...........1

O

HELEN O'GRADY...........4

P

LUKE PEARSON...........

Photo: Joanna Briggs Photography / www.joannabphotography.co.uk

PROJECT FOUR

pallet order of the day

Order of the days are a great way of letting your guests know the running order of your big day. They are especially handy if you have younger guests who will be eager to know when they get to eat, or how long they have to sit still for! A really simple way to display an order of the day is using an old reclaimed pallet. You can often find them advertised quite cheaply on Facebook marketplace, or alternatively at local wood reclaim yards. Avoid any painted pallets as these usually have been used with chemicals and instead stick to plain wooden ones.

SUPPLIES

Old wooden pallet

Sanding sheet

Chalk (optional)

Small round paintbrush

Paint (choose exterior friendly paint if using outdoors)

PROCESS

1/ Begin by cleaning down your pallet, they can usually be a bit dirty and rough so sand down any sharp areas to smooth the surface as much as possible. If you wish you can also stain your pallet, but the bare look works really well, especially for rustic weddings!

2/ Using a piece of chalk, write out your desired wording on each slat. Once you are happy, use your paintbrush and paint to paint over the chalk lines. If you are using the pallet outdoors, use exterior wood paint to ensure it is weatherproof. You can also add a little bit of water to your paint to help you get a more fluid motion with the paintbrush.

3/ Once the paint is dry you can use a damp cloth to remove any leftover chalk residue.

PROJECT FIVE

leather jacket

Personalised jackets have been a popular trend for some time now, and they are such a cool alternative to covering up on your big day. Painted leather jackets are definitely the most popular choice when it comes to personalised jackets, and using my ever so favourite POSCA pen, they can be quite easy to create yourself.

SUPPLIES

Leather jacket
Scrap paper and pencil
Chalk
Low talk masking tape
Ball-point Pen
Uni POSCA Marker
Dry Cloth
Hairdryer

PROCESS

1/ Begin by wiping down your jacket to ensure the surface is clean and allow to dry thoroughly.

2/ On scrap paper, draw out your design to the size you want on your jacket. Once happy, turn the paper over and cover the paper in a layer of chalk.

3/ Place the paper, chalk side down, onto the jacket in the position you want your design. You can secure the design in low tack masking tape if required.

4/ Using a ball-point pen, trace over your design. Press hard enough to transfer the chalk through to the jacket. Once finished, carefully remove the paper design from the jacket to reveal your design in chalk.

5/ Trace over your chalk guides with a Uni POSCA marker and allow to dry. I recommend working upwards to prevent your hands rubbing away the chalk marks as you write.

6/ Once the lettering is dry, use a dry cloth to rub away any remaining chalk. Use a hairdryer and dry the design for 30 seconds which will set the pen into the leather.

PROJECT SIX

fabric banner

Fabric banners make a wonderful option for wedding signage, particularly if you are getting married abroad and need something that is easy to transport. They work perfectly for backdrops, as well as seat banners, welcome signs, or general quotes and instructions for guests, to add personality to your venue. Lettering on fabric does require some practice, the key is making sure you get your fabric tight to stop it moving around. It's always a good idea to practice on some scrap fabric before working on your final piece. Some sewing experience is also recommended for this tutorial.

SUPPLIES

100% Calico Fabric
Scrap paper and pencil
Tailors (fabric) chalk
Carbon transfer paper (optional)
Black POSCA Pen
Scrap piece of card
Thread and needle/sewing machine
Wooden Dowel
Cord for hanging

A standard cutting template has been added as a download in to our members only lettering community for you to use or adapt as you wish.
www.facebook.com/groups/hscletteringcommunity

PROCESS

1/ Begin by downloading our free cutting template, or using this to create your own. Cut 2 pieces in your fabric of the same size (front and back) which will eventually be sewn together. Sketch out your design on the template or some scrap paper.

2/ Set one of the pieces aside, and on the other, sketch out your design with tailors chalk. This is special chalk that writes on fabric, and can be removed or washed off once finished. Alternatively, you can carefully trace your design onto the fabric using carbon transfer paper if you prefer.

3/ Place the scrap piece of cardboard behind your fabric, and using your POSCA pen, slowly trace over your design. The cardboard helps adds stability to your fabric making it easier to write on. Once the paint has dried, iron the back of the design to set the paint.

4/ Place the back piece over the top of your design (so the design is on the inside). Sew together all of the edges except the top to join together and turn through. Iron the edges flat on the back side, and then fold over the top to create a loop for your wooden dowel and sew to secure.

5/ Push your dowel through the loop. Drill a hole 1cm from the edge of each end, thread through the cord, and tie to secure.

Photo: Foyetography / www.foyetography.co.uk

RESOURCES AND RECOMMENDATIONS

Below is a list of recommended suppliers and resources of materials for further learning. I have also included a list of recommended lettering artists, all of whom have provided me with some amazing inspiration throughout my lettering journey.

TOOLS AND SUPPLIES

Cass Art
www.cassart.co.uk

Scribblers
www.scribblers.co.uk

POSCA
www.posca.com

Blots Pen & Ink Supplies
www.blotspens.co.uk

Cult Pens
www.cultpens.com

The Calligraphy Store
www.thecalligraphystore.com

The Range
www.therange.co.uk

PAPER SUPPLIERS

GF Smith
www.gfsmith.com

PDA Card & Craft
www.pdacardandcraft.co.uk

PROJECT MATERIALS

Wood Craft Shapes
www.woodcraftshapes.co.uk

Baker Ross
www.bakerross.co.uk

B&Q (Plywood cut to size)
www.diy.com

IKEA (wooden crates, photo frames)
www.ikea.co.uk

Etsy (acrylic blanks)
www.etsy.co.uk

Hobbycraft
www.hobbycraft.co.uk

Community Wood Recycling (reclaimed pallets)
www.communitywoodrecycling.org.uk

FURTHER LEARNING RESOURCES

Beginners Guide to Modern Lettering Community
www.facebook.com/groups/hscletteringcommunity

Skillshare
www.skillshare.com

LETTERING ARTISTS

Rebecca Cahill / Betty Etiquette
www.bettyetiquette.co.uk

Lauren Hom – Hom Sweet Hom
www.homsweethom.com

Little Red Bird Love
www.instagram.com/littleredbirdlove

Peggy Dean – The Pigeon Letters
www.thepigeonletters.com

Shelly Kim – Letters by Shells
www.lettersbyshells.com

Chalked by Mabz
www.chalkedbymabz.com

The Letterettes
www.instagram.com/theletterettes

Stefan Kunz
www.stefankunz.com

Nicole Miyuki Santo
www.nicolemiyuki.com

ACKNOWLEDGEMENTS

I am incredibly lucky to have the most amazing and incredibly supportive group of family and friends who have not only helped me with the creation of this book, but also with my business. Thank you to my family for always supporting everything I do, and helping with childcare when I needed to take time to grow my business. Thank you to my husband for always giving me the courage and belief that I can achieve what I want, and standing by me through all the tough times during my battle with PND. Thank you to my wonderful friends for always believing in me. I would also like to say a massive thank you to the brilliant Matt Glover for his incredible photography skills as well as all of the other photographers who have kindly allowed me to use their work in this book; Joanna Briggs, Stephanie Butt, and Sky Photography. And finally, a special, thank you to my girls, Sofia and Helena, for just being you, I love you more than words could ever say.

Credits by page:
PAGE 3 / Photography: www.mattgloverphotography.co.uk PAGE 5 / Photography: www.mattgloverphotography.co.uk
PAGE 6 / Photography: www.stephaniebutt.com / Styling: www.thetwohummingbirds.co.uk PAGE 11 / Photography:
www.mattgloverphotography.co.uk PAGE 12 / Photography: www.joannabphotography.co.uk / Cake: www.daintybakes.co.uk
PAGE 16 / Photography: www.pearbearphotography.com / Couple: Dani and Matt PAGE 20 / Photography:
www.skyphotography.co.uk / Couple: Lucy and Matt PAGE 40 / Photography: www.majatsolo.com / Couple: Zoe and Dan
PAGE 48 / Photography: www.stephaniebutt.com / Styling: www.thetwohummingbirds.co.uk PAGE 54 / Photography:
www.joannabphotography.co.uk / Props: www.chattelier.com / Styling: www.tulleandblue.co.uk / Flowers: www.damsonandvine.com
PAGE 58 / Photography: www.joannabphotography.co.uk / Flowers: www.damsonandvine.com PAGE 67 / Photography:
www.mattgloverphotography.co.uk PAGE 68 / Photography: www.mattgloverphotography.co.uk PAGE 71 / Photography:
www.skyphotography.co.uk / Couple: Lucy and Matt PAGE 73 / Photography: www.joannabphotography.co.uk / Props:
www.chattelier.com / Styling: www.tulleandblue.co.uk / Flowers: www.damsonandvine.com / Candle Favour: www.etsy.com/people/
fivebeesyard PAGE 75 / Photography: www.joannabphotography.co.uk / Flowers: www.damsonandvine.com
PAGE 77 / Photography: www.joannabphotography.co.uk / Flowers: www.damsonandvine.com / Venue: www.hommehouse.co.uk
PAGE 81 / Photography: www.mattgloverphotography.co.uk PAGE 82 / Photography: www.foyetography.co.uk / Venue:
www.thegiraffeshed.com / Flowers: www.instagram.com/hazefloral / Styling: www.instagram.com/randrweddingsandevents

INDEX